WEIRD AND WONDERFUL
SHIPS

Published 1975 by Enterprise Books
Secausus, New Jersey

Copyright © 1975 by Intercontinental Book Productions
Library of Congress Catalog Card Number 74–24828

ISBN 0–89009–031–9

Printed and bound in Belgium

WEIRD AND WONDERFUL
SHIPS

Written by Graeme Cook
Illustrated by R. A. Sherrington
John Wood and Brian Watson
Cover illustration Brian Edwards

ENTERPRISE BOOKS

Contents

Introduction

Of all forms of transport, water-borne craft are among those which have been around the longest. Staggering changes have been made in the design of ships and boats over these thousands of years. In the evolution of vessels there have appeared from time to time some remarkably peculiar craft — some ridiculous, others splendid and magnificent.

In the history of ships, which ranges from the first dug-out canoe to the nuclear-powered ocean-going ship of today, we have selected craft both weird and wonderful, some conceived by 'crack-pot' inventors, others born in the minds of brilliant men whose contribution to ships and shipping has made sea-voyaging what it is today. They are here to enjoy and marvel at in the pages that follow . . .

The dug-out canoe, which is said to date back as far as 6000 BC, was the successor to the floating log, which Man first used to support himself on water. Made from a felled tree trunk, the cavity was gouged out of it by using primitive stone axes and fire. This type of craft was found where trees flourished, and dug-outs, not unlike this one, are still used in some of the less advanced parts of the world

The First Boats

When and where Man first took to the water in boats is a mystery, and one which is likely to remain unsolved. We can only guess that he began by swimming many thousands of years ago and progressed to the use of primitive craft, beginning the evolution of the boat and ship.

Throughout the world, where streams, rivers, lakes or land-locked seas existed, Man found a means of transporting himself upon the water. How he did it was determined by the raw materials for building which were to be found in the country around him. Where trees were plentiful, he felled logs which would float and support his weight, and used his hands as paddles. Then he went a step further, lashing logs together to form a raft, or hacking the inside out of a log to make the first canoe. As time went on he invented crude paddles to propel himself across the water.

In other parts of the world, like along the banks of the River Nile, papyrus grass grew in abundance, and the Egyptians built rafts out of this buoyant material. Balsa, a very light wood, was also used extensively in raft building. But perhaps

Dug-out canoe

Where wood or other naturally buoyant materials were not plentiful, Man found that an inflated animal skin, internally reinforced with a skeleton framework, would float and carry the weight of a man. He was quick to adopt this as a means of transporting himself on water.

Inflated animal skin

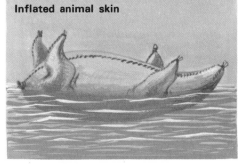

Trees were scarce along the banks of the River Nile, so the Egyptians used bundles of papyrus lashed together to form small rafts. With the advent of sail, much bigger papyrus rafts were built and used extensively on the Nile.

One of the earliest water craft was the hobolo, the hull of which was fashioned out of ambatch wood. It was propelled by a long pole. This type of craft has survived thousands of years and is still in use on Lake Abaya, in Ethiopia.

Hobolo

Papyrus raft

the most ingenious form of early water transport was inflated animal skins. By sewing skins tightly together to form a leak-proof bag, early man could inflate it and ride upon it across the water. In some parts of the world these strange craft are still in use. Likewise, the small one-man coracle, fashioned out of wicker covered with animal skin, is in use today for salmon fishing in some rivers of Wales. In places as far apart as

The jangada fishing boat, which is still used in some parts of Brazil, is thought to have existed 6000 years ago. Its hull is formed of logs bound together. To make the craft more stable, a crude keel juts below the waterline amidships.

Jangada

Lake Abaya, in Ethiopia, and Brazil, boats of the type which were in use thousands of years ago are in operation.

The coming of sail and oars revolutionized water transport. Bigger boats and ships were built with these new means of propulsion. It was then that some of the truly great craft of these early times made their appearance. Records exist showing these vessels, particularly those which plied the waters of the Mediterranean Sea. By about 3000 BC the Egyptians had advanced from the use of papyrus to building their ships of short wooden planks of acacia or sycamore, the only types of wood available to them. Using these more sea-worthy craft, they

Coracle

The coracle dates back many thousands of years, but it is still used by salmon fishermen on rivers in parts of Wales. It is built by making a framework of withes (willows) and covering it with stretched animal skins. It originated in areas where trees were scarce and dug-out canoes could not be made.

Greek war galley

The Greeks are better known now as merchant seamen than fighting sailors, but long ago things were quite different. They engaged in some fierce sea battles in ships like the galley shown here. Their war galleys varied in both size and design and were known as biremes, triremes or quadremes, indicating two, three or four sets of rowers.

At the Battle of Salamis in 480 BC, a fleet of 1,000 Persian ships engaged a mere 300 Greek triremes and biremes, but the smaller force dealt the Persians a mortal blow and defeated them.

The Phoenicians of the eastern Mediterranean were among the greatest of the early sailors. They built two quite distinct types of ship: the long ship (seen here), designed for fighting and equipped with pointed rams for sinking enemy vessels, and round ships, without rams or fighting decks and used for trading and carrying cargo. Both types originated around 500 BC.

The Arab dhow in its varied form has survived centuries, changing little in basic design and remaining an unusual ship with towering, pointed sails roughly triangular in shape and dominating the hull. It was in a dhow like this one that the Arabs sailed the Indian Ocean in times past.

Phoenician long ship

forged out into the Mediterranean, trading with other countries. During these expeditions, they bought cedar wood with which they built bigger and more robust ships. By 1500 BC, they had built ships which incorporated keels.

With these new ships the Egyptians showed their prowess as seamen when Queen Hatshepsut provisioned two ships for what was then a considerable voyage to Somalia.

They were not alone in their sea-faring. The Phoenicians, who lived in the land now called Lebanon, became great sailors, building both their long ships

Kon Tiki

Balsa wood, a very light and buoyant material, was used extensively in the building of boats in Ancient times. In 1950 Thor Heyerdahl, a Norwegian explorer, built the balsa wood boat Kon Tiki (seen here) and sailed it 4,300 miles across the Pacific from South America to Tahiti, thus proving that Polynesians could have made a similar voyage in the same type of boat some 1,500 years earlier.

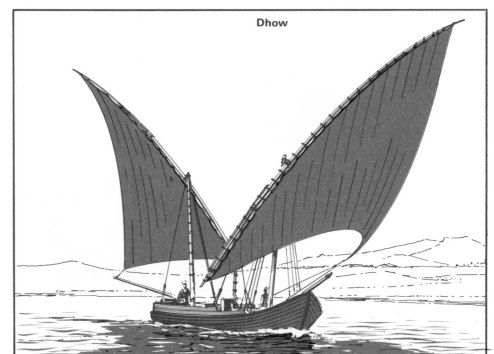

Dhow

and round ships. Other nations copied their designs and the inevitable sea battles began in the Mediterranean.

The long ships of the Phoenicians were the fighting vessels, equipped with fierce-looking pointed rams with which they sank enemy ships. Long, narrow fighting decks spanned the length of the ship above the heads of the rowers, and soldiers fought from there. The Greeks too had their fighting galleys, and the Romans followed suit, copying the designs of the Phoenician ships but adding 'castles' on deck either in front of or behind the mast. The reason for the addition of the castle is not clear.

In the North Sea, Viking long ships made lightning raids on the coast of Britain. These were open sailing boats in which the crew had to brave the rigors of foul weather with no protection. Each of the oarsmen sat on a skin-covered

Viking raiding ship

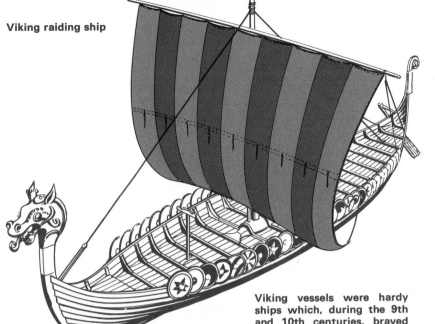

Viking vessels were hardy ships which, during the 9th and 10th centuries, braved the rigors of the North Sea, carrying raiders to pillage and plunder Britain. Their grotesque figureheads gave them a fierce appearance, not unlike that of the men who sailed them.

Foochow Chinese junk

seat which housed his food and weapons. It was in ships like this that the Vikings sailed to Iceland, Greenland and America.

Among adventurers from warmer climes were the Arabs, who ventured forth in their dhows, small boats with huge triangular lateen sails of the type which are used in modern yachts. These dhows can still be seen on the Nile.

Farther afield in the Far East, Chinese junks with their ribbed sails and angular lines plied the seas on trading and fishing trips.

Malayan fishing raft

Although then still a primitive race, the Maoris of New Zealand produced some fine vessels. Their war canoes, long, fast and intricately decorated, could carry up to 60 warriors. The larger tainui, a twin-hulled sea-going Maori craft, made remarkable ocean voyages over long stretches of the Pacific.

The Malayan fishing raft and the Irawadi rice boat, both born in the Dark Ages, have changed little from those far-off days and are still used — a fitting tribute to those who designed them so long ago.

Patile sailing boat

This Malayan fishing raft, with its catching net suspended on a boom, is still in use in parts of the Malay Archipelago. Made of bamboo cane, it has altered little in design since its inception many hundreds of years ago.

The Foochow Chinese junk, with its ribbed sails and ornate embellishment, can still be seen plying the China Seas. Like the other forms of junk, it has changed little in 500 years.

The patile sailing boat has been used on the River Ganges for hundreds of years. It is a dual-purpose craft, used both as a cargo vessel and house-boat. Its most unusual feature is the large side rudder for steering.

Men O' War

The Great Harry, or *Henry Grace a Dieu* as she was also known, was built in 1514 in record time for England's Henry VIII. She was unquestionably the greatest ship of her day, displacing 1,500 tons and with a length of 200 feet. The Great Harry had two fore and aft decks surmounted by two castles. Armed with 21 muzzle-loading guns and more than 230 smaller weapons, she was the most formidable warship of that era.

Perhaps the toughest, most bloody battles fought at sea were those in which the most splendid ships took part. Ships of almost all the warring maritime nations were magnificent vessels, heavily armed, colorful and ornately decorated. But cannon ball and pointed ram wrought dreadful destruction upon enemy ships. In those days, when the sailing or oar-driven warship sailed the seas, close combat was the order of the day. Boarding parties clashed in gory hand-to-hand conflict with cutlass and musket.

Great Harry

Despite the grace and beauty of these warships, the conditions under which the ordinary seaman had to live were unbelievably bad. Discipline was cruelly strict and the food rarely fit even for common swine. Scurvy was rife through lack of fresh green food and often took a greater toll of men than the fierce battles themselves. Ships' surgeons neither cared nor had the skill to minister to the ills and wounds of the crew. Life for the seamen of those far-off days was bad. Yet there is a feeling of romance for that distant era — the day of the cutlass, the cannon and the man o' war.

There can be little envy for the seaman, but his ship was a sight to behold. The *Great Harry*, built for England's King Henry VIII, inspired awe in all who saw her. She was the greatest ship of her day, heavily armed and built in record time, yet she was found to be incapable of ocean travel because of her complex sail arrangement and the weight of her guns. She ended life ignominiously in

Sovereign of the Seas

Turkish galley

The Sovereign of the Seas; of 1637 vintage and built in Britain, has justifiably been hailed as 'the most beautiful ship ever built.' Nicknamed 'The Golden Devil' by the Dutch because of her decoration and fire-power, she was a masterpiece of design by two brothers, Peter and Phineas Pett. One of the first ships to have three decks, she cost $150,000 to build, a veritable fortune in those days. She was armed with 100 cannon, which roared in many battles.

This Turkish galley took part in the greatest ever galley battle at Lepanto in 1571. Powered by both sail and oars, she mounted a single cannon by the ram at her bows. Her towering stern gave her the appearance of being out of balance.

An internal view shows a typical English galleon of the type which routed the Spanish Armada in 1588. Although the officers lived in comparative luxury, the ordinary seamen suffered the most appalling conditions aboard these ships. The three-gun decks with their gun ports had to be located well above the waterline to avoid the sea gushing in through the ports when the ship rolled in heavy seas.

The Victory, flagship of Horatio Nelson, is the most famous warship ever built. With a displacement of over 2,000 tons, she carried 104 guns and took 19 years to build, from 1759 to 1778. It was in this great ship that Admiral Nelson was mortally wounded at the Battle of Trafalgar. As a token of respect for both ship and Admiral, Victory has been preserved and is open to the public at Portsmouth, England.

1552 when she caught fire and was burnt out.

Ships of countries at the eastern end of the Mediterranean preferred to retain their oarsmen as auxiliary power to drive their warships. Turkish galleys, although sporting a cannon, shunned the idea of relinquishing their pointed rams which could pierce an enemy ship's side.

The year 1637 saw the launching of the warship which, it was claimed, was the most beautiful ship ever built. She was the *Sovereign of the Seas* and she certainly lived up to her reputation as a ship the British could be proud of. Her 100 cannon made her a formidable opponent for a foe, but she was a costly ship to build. She is estimated to have cost around $150,000 to complete – not much when one considers that it costs millions to build a modern warship, but a fortune in her day.

Although warships had to be practical and efficient fighting vessels in those days of the 16th, 17th and 18th centuries, they had also, the designers believed, to be works of art to look at. The British Navy's *Royal William* incorporated both these requisites and more. Her carved stern would have done justice to any great sculptor. But she was far from being merely a show-piece. She was built of solid stuff and remained in service with the British Navy for almost 100 years.

No one could doubt that the most famous ship ever built in Britain is Admiral Nelson's *Victory*. This 104-gun flagship, displacing more than 2,000 tons, took almost 20 years to build.

It was on the deck of this great ship, while in the thick of the Battle of Trafalgar, that a sniper's bullet mortally wounded Britain's greatest admiral. As a mark of respect, and as a monument to both the admiral and those 'romantic' days of fighting sail, *Victory* has been preserved at Portsmouth, England, for all to see.

The mid-19th century saw the beginning of the end of the sailing warship when steam engines were introduced into the ships of the line. Although changing little in general outward appearance, they sprouted funnels and bore screws or propellers to thrust them through calm waters. Ships like the 92-gun Frenchman *Napoleon* became the first major warships to incorporate a steam engine and propeller. The onset of a revolution was at hand and the era of fighting sail was grinding to a halt with growing certainty.

Napoleon

The Napoleon, built in France in 1852, was the first major ship of the line to be equipped with both steam and propeller. She retained her sail but her funnels looked curiously out of place on a ship which more closely resembled the older men o' war. Carrying 92 guns, she displaced 5,057 tons and was powered by a 900-hp steam engine which could make 14 knots.

The magnificence of men o' war in the 17th and 18th centuries must have been a glory to behold. Their builders were artists as well as craftsmen and this stern view of the Royal William bears witness to that. She served with the English Navy for almost 100 years, from 1719 to 1813.

The *Affondatore* was built in Britain in 1865 for the Italian Navy. She combined both steam and sail, and although she carried two 10-inch guns mounted in turrets, she was designed essentially as a ram with her jutting iron bow. *Affondatore* failed to prove her worth when she was badly damaged during the Battle of Lissa in 1866.

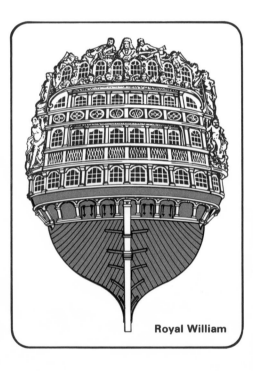

Royal William

Affondatore

The New Warship

The Greek *Karteria* earned a place in the history of warfare by becoming the first steamship to see action at sea. This small vessel with her towering funnel was lightly armed with eight small-caliber guns. Although equipped with sail, she used only her steam power when she clashed with six Turkish ships in 1826 and sank all of them by gunfire.

Karteria

One of the most unusual — and useless — ships ever to be built was the Russian *Novgorod,* nicknamed 'Pop-Offka.' Completed in 1873, she was circular in shape with a 101-foot diameter. Armed with two 12-inch guns, she was hopelessly uncontrollable. She was flat bottomed and her deck rose only 1½ feet above the waterline.

As long ago as 1826, there came the first hint of revolutionary change in warship design. The Greek paddle-driven steamship *Karteria,* although equipped with sail, became the first steamship to see action at sea. Armed with only eight small-caliber guns, she routed and sank no fewer than six Turkish ships — and she achieved this victory over her adversaries while using only her steam power. None of the enemy ships had the advantage of steam power, and in a windless sea the *Karteria* ran rings around them, picking off her targets at will. The encounter was a significant one, for it proved without doubt the advantage of the steam engine in a warship. No longer was the warship dependent upon the elements in time of battle.

By the mid-19th century, the navies of Britain, France and America had followed suit and installed steam engines in their mighty ships of the line. They retained their then conventional shapes,

Novgorod

Monitor

Devastation

like great 100-gun hulks with towering masts sporting sail, but added to that were funnels and propellers. No longer had they to rely exclusively upon the eccentricities of the wind when engaged in a clash with the enemy. But even these floating behemoths had their disadvantages — they were built of wood, and however strong it might have been it was still vulnerable to cannon-fire.

The tougher, iron-built ship could withstand infinitely greater punishment — and this then became the warship of the future. The new all-iron ship was the ideal vessel for the warship builder — and what a weird assortment of craft evolved from this concept.

Among those early, heavily armored ships was the American Federal Navy's 'ironclad' Monitor, an unusual vessel in appearance because she lay so low in the water. But she incorporated one outstanding innovation — a *revolving* turret sporting two 11-inch guns. No longer had the ship to manoeuvre to fire a broadside at her enemy — she had simply to turn her turret to unleash her shells. She had one further advantage: she lay so low in the water that, especially at night, she was an extremely difficult ship to see.

During the American Civil War, the Monitor and its Confederate States counterpart, the Merrimac, engaged in a minor scuffle during an encounter

Britain was the first naval power to depart completely from the use of sail in her warships with the introduction of the ironclad Devastation in 1873. Armed with torpedo tubes and four 10-inch guns, this armor-plated vessel set the pattern for the great warships of all the major naval powers of the world.

Dreadnought

She was a shipbuilder's nightmare, circular in shape with a diameter of 101 feet, armed with two 12-inch guns and utterly uncontrollable at sea because of her flat bottom. Her deck must have been almost always awash, for it rose only 1½ feet above the waterline.

But the warship to change all fighting ships arrived in 1906, when the British battleship *Dreadnought* slid down the slipway. Driven by turbine engines and armed with ten 12-inch guns, eight of which she could use at one time to fire a broadside, she alone pointed the way for the huge battleships of the future. *Dreadnought* did, however, have two more formidable aids to her armory; jutting bows which could slice through a smaller ship with ease, and five torpedo tubes which, fired accurately, could tear an enemy ship apart.

Battleships, armored ships, heavy and light cruisers, as well as the smaller destroyers, evolved into striking seaborne weapons during and after the First World War. Then came the Second World War, and with it infinitely more powerful warships . . .

The giant builders were the navies of the Axis (German and Japanese) forces. The Germans built some huge ships, like *Tirpitz* and *Bismarck*, but it was their allies, the Japanese, who built the giant to beat them all — the battleship *Yamato*. Launched when completed in 1942, *Yamato* was the biggest and most powerful battleship ever built. She had a displacement of around 64,000 tons and an overall length of 863 feet. But despite her enormous size she could make a speed of 27 knots. She had a staggering number of small-caliber weapons, but her offensive teeth lay in her nine 18·1-inch and twelve 6·1-inch heavy guns. All this was supplemented by the six aircraft she could carry. But the bigger they come the harder they fall, and in 1945 she was sent to the bottom by

Built in 1906, the British Dreadnought was the first battleship to be turbine driven. But more than that she was the prototype for the great battleships that followed. Her jutting bows were reminiscent of the rams of the ancient war galleys found in the Mediterranean. She was capable of firing a broadside from eight of her ten 12-inch guns. Dreadnought was also equipped with five torpedo tubes.

The Japanese were renowned for their mighty surface and submarine ships. The biggest and most powerful of them all was the battleship Yamato, completed in 1942. She had a displacement of 64,000 tons, was 863 feet long, and could make 27·7 knots. Among her bristling fire-power were nine 18·1-inch and twelve 6·1-inch guns. She could also carry six aircraft.

at sea. But neither ship sustained any damage. Both these ships were quite small; too minute, in fact, to engage in the accepted large-scale battles at sea.

It was the British navy which, after due consideration, decided to dispense completely with sail in her warships, and the ironclad *Devastation*, which operated solely under steam power, was launched in 1873. The turning point had come. *Devastation*, with a displacement of 9,330 tons, had an iron hull and supplementary armor plating to protect her against shelling. Four 10-inch guns in rotating turrets gave her her 'punch,' while two torpedo tubes added to her potency. She set a pattern in warship design which other navies were quick to follow.

In that same epoch-making year, the Russians launched one of the most ridiculous craft ever to take to the water. She was the gunboat *Novgorod*, which aptly gained the nickname 'Popoffka.'

Yamato

Fearless

HMS Fearless is one of the British Navy's most versatile ships, specially built for amphibious warfare. She is equipped as a Naval Assault Ship and Brigade Headquarters from which naval and military personnel can work in close co-operation. A flight deck at the stern is used by assault helicopters. Tank Landing Craft are housed in the ship's dry dock and can be launched from her open-ended stern.

eleven torpedoes and seven bomb hits from American aircraft.

The modern day warship bears little resemblance to these giants of the past, but they carry a more formidable punch with their guided missiles and highly-sophisticated equipment.

Among the more unusual ships in service today is the Royal Navy's HMS *Fearless*, a multi-role Naval Assault Ship designed for amphibious warfare. Not only does she act as a naval and military headquarters, but she incorporates a flight deck for helicopters to take commandos on raids, and a dry dock from which Tank Landing Craft can be launched.

The whole concept of war at sea has changed, and with it the ships to fit the purpose.

17

Submarines

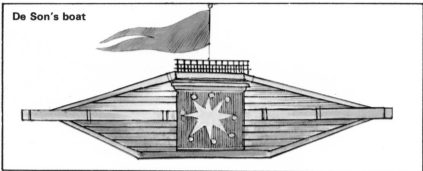

De Son's boat

In 1653, the Dutch designer De Son built this spindle-shaped craft. Trials were carried out at Rotterdam, where it is said to have submerged.

This inside view of Bushnell's submersible craft, Turtle, shows the many controls its crewman had to operate. Built by David Bushnell in 1775, it carried out an unsuccessful attack on a British warship in New York harbor. The Turtle carried an explosive charge which could be attached to a warship. All its underwater movements were controlled by hand-powered screws. It was the first craft to contain a tank at the bottom for buoyancy control.

In the course of its development, the submarine has taken on some truly remarkable shapes. The possibility of voyaging beneath the sea intrigued ship builders for many centuries. It is said that Alexander the Great, who died in 323 BC, explored the Mediterranean sea bed in a glass barrel and took a chicken with him 'to guarantee a safe return.' How long he is supposed to have remained submerged is a mystery.

The Catalan Bell, said to have been used for the recovery of wreckage from

Bushnell's Turtle

the depths in 1600 AD, was lowered into the water from two boats. It remained submerged for as long as the 'captured' fresh air in the bell lasted.

Twenty years later King James I witnessed the first display of a submarine when the Dutchman Cornelius van Drebbel sailed his craft in the Thames. The king must have been impressed, for he too took a trip in it. The submarine was built of well-oiled leather stretched over a wooden framework and carried a crew of 12 oarsmen who propelled it under the water. It could not have been a great success for nothing more was heard of it.

In 1653, another Dutchman, De Son, built a spindle-shaped submersible which is said to have been capable of underwater travel. Then in 1775 came Bushnell's *Turtle*, which was the first submersible craft to be used as an offensive weapon. It was not until the 19th century, however, that anything vaguely resembling today's submarines arrived on the scene with the coming of Fulton's *Nautilus* and Bauer's submarine *Le Diable Marin*.

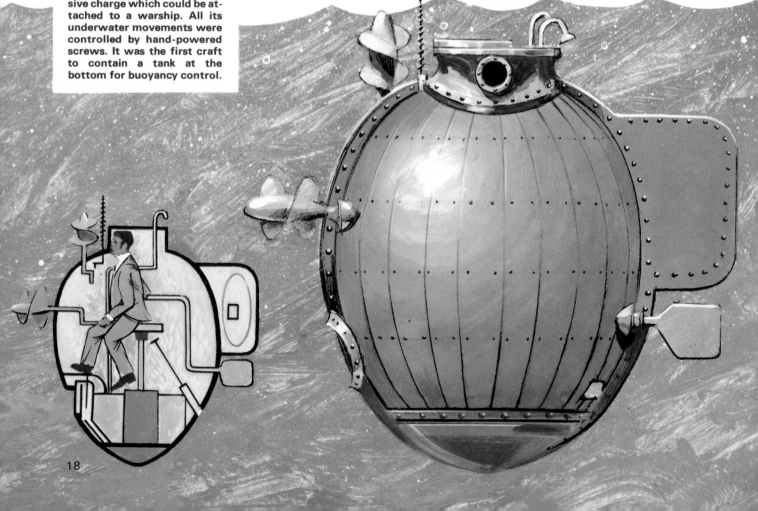

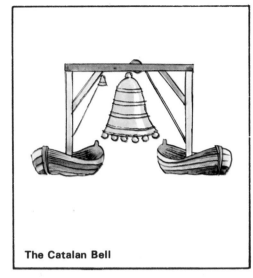

The Catalan Bell

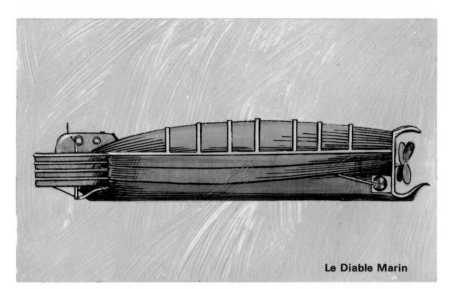

Le Diable Marin

Designers of these craft encountered many problems, not the least of which was actually staying alive underwater, and tragedies were commonplace. It was not unusual for a submarine to disappear beneath the waves and never be seen again. A willingness to sacrifice one's life was demanded of all these early inventors.

A classic example of the hazards of submarine travel came to light during the American Civil War, when the *Hunley* was used by the Confederate Navy. This eight-man submarine hit problems during its early trials, and indeed sank no fewer than five times, on each occasion losing most of its crew. Thirty-five men lost their lives during these trials, but despite this there was never any lack of volunteers to go down in her.

Built in 1600 of wood bound with iron, the Catalan Bell diving bell was used for the recovery of wreckage from the seabed. The crew could remain submerged for the short periods that the fresh air 'captured' in the bell lasted.

Called *Le Diable Marin*, Bauer's submarine was operated by the use of propellers, which were driven by two of the three-man crew. To celebrate the coronation of the Tsar of Russia in 1855, Bauer took *Le Diable Marin* underwater with a four-piece orchestra on board. It is said that the music could be heard on the surface.

Built in 1801 and made of copper, John Fulton's Nautilus incorporated a ballast tank and hydroplanes to control its depth. For surface power, it was fitted with a collapsible sail and mast.

Fulton's Nautilus

Built by the American Simon Lake in 1899, the *Argonaut* could travel on the sea bed by means of large wheels attached to it. A special trap door allowed wreckage to be recovered from the depths of the sea. Port-holes made of thick glass gave the crew limited underwater vision.

Argonaut

Production of the K-class submarine began during the First World War. Steam powered on the surface, she had a high surface speed, but her funnels had to be lowered before she could dive. Unfortunately she suffered a disastrous history. Six were lost in accidents, five cancelled, four converted and the others being built were scrapped.

The eight-man crew of the Hunley provided the 'power' to drive it while submerged. Used by the American Confederate Navy during the Civil War, it sank five times before getting into action. A total of 35 lives were lost in its use.

Hunley

K-class submarine

It was not until 1875, when the American John Holland drew up plans for his *Holland 1*, that the first practical submarine made its appearance. Holland incorporated two forms of power; steam for driving the craft on the surface and a battery-powered electric motor for submerged travel. Although surface motive power was to change, the *Holland* formed the basic design for the successful submarines of the future.

In 1899, another American, Simon Lake, invented an odd-looking submarine which was primarily a recovery vessel, used to salvage wreckage from the sea bed and to carry out voyages of exploration. Equipped with portholes which permitted limited underwater vision, its most unusual feature was two large wheels upon which it could ride along the bottom of the sea.

Submarines equipped with torpedoes came into their own during the First World War when they were used with devastating effect by the Germans against British shipping. But even then they had their drawbacks; they were slow, even on the surface, and it was this factor which prompted the Royal Navy to introduce the K-class steam-powered submarine. The requirement was for a submarine capable of operating with the fleet, which meant a surface cruising speed in excess of 20 knots. And in those days only steam power could drive a submarine at such speed. Unfortunately the installation of steam engines into the K-class submarine sparked off a trail of disasters. Six of these craft were lost in accidents with a fearful loss of life. Not surprisingly, none of the K-class boats saw action.

Until the coming of the nuclear-powered submarine, the conventional underwater craft was powered by diesel engines for surface travel and electric motors for operations beneath the sea. Armed with torpedoes and deck guns, these submarines proved highly effective weapons.

There were still, however, the oddities, like the French submarine cruiser *Surcouf*. Launched in 1929, she was the biggest underwater craft of her time. She had an underwater displacement of no fewer than 4,304 tons, but her most unusual features were the two heavy 8-inch guns mounted in a turret, and her ability to carry a seaplane for reconnaissance. The intention was to use her on long-distance sorties against enemy shipping. She could cruise for 90 days without refuelling and had accommodation for 40 prisoners.

Surcouf

The French *Surcouf*, launched in 1929, was a submarine cruiser, and one of the biggest underwater craft of its time. She was 361 feet long and had a submerged displacement of 4,304 tons. Armed with two 8-inch guns in a twin turret, she also had twelve torpedo tubes. She carried a seaplane, could cruise for 90 days, and even had space for 40 prisoners.

Torpedo Boats

Torpedo sloop

The origins of the torpedo boat date back a little more than 100 years to the time when a 'brave' inventor built a torpedo sloop. The craft was simply an ordinary small boat with a long spar attachment stretching out in front of it. At the end of this spar was a bomb with which it was hoped to ram the enemy ship and inflict a mortal wound. It takes little imagination to realize that if the bomb were powerful enough to severely damage the enemy warship, it would also blow the torpedo sloop to bits with its blast.

With the coming of the torpedo as we know it today — a long cigar-shaped

This Torpedo sloop, as it was known, undoubtedly held greater danger for its crew than for the ship it was attacking. Built for the American Confederate States Navy in 1861, it had an explosive bomb at the end of a long pole. The intention was to strike the enemy warship with the bomb, whereupon the 'torpedo' would explode. The Torpedo sloop bore no resemblance to the torpedo boat as we know it today.

Coastal Motor Boat

The small, fast Coastal Motor Boat of the Royal Navy saw service during the First World War. Powered by a gasoline engine, this type could make between 30 and 40 knots. It carried a torpedo housed in a 'trough' aft, and was launched backwards over the stern. The four drums seen on deck were depth charges for use against submarines.

Motoscafi Anti-Sommergibile

The element of surprise was the object behind this unusually fast Italian torpedo boat, designated *Motoscafi Anti-Sommergibile*. First built in 1917 and powered by almost silent electric motors, its role was essentially against submarines. It was armed with two torpedoes and anti-submarine bombs.

The British MTB 74 of the Second World War was an unusual craft, fickle in her performance. Powered by five engines, which refused to work in concert with each other, she could either travel at a mere 6 knots or dash at 40 knots. Unfortunately she would not cruise at any speeds in between. Furthermore her two torpedo tubes were mounted on the fore deck, unlike almost every other type of MTB.

weapon with a high-explosive warhead — the requirement was for a fast surface craft to deliver the torpedo in an attack on enemy warships. Speed, and with it the element of surprise, was of the essence if torpedo boats were to be really effective.

In the First World War, the Royal Navy used their fast Coastal Motor Boats, equipped with torpedoes which were launched backwards over the stern of the boat.

Later in that same war, the Italians, ever conscious of the need for surprise, built the *Motoscafi Anti-Sommergibile*, an electrically-powered boat which was almost silent.

In the Second World War, Motor Torpedo Boats did valiant work against enemy shipping, particularly in the waters around Britain, in the Mediterranean, and, using the American version, the PT Boat, in the Pacific.

Perhaps the most unusual torpedo boat of the Second World War was MTB 74, with its fo'c's'le-mounted tubes. She achieved the dubious distinction of being able to travel at only two speeds, either 6 knots or 40 knots, making her a singularly difficult vessel to handle. Despite her obvious drawbacks, however, she successfully took part in one of the greatest combined operations of the war — the Raid on St. Nazaire.

MTB 74

Aircraft Carriers

Manxman

Since building specially designed ships for the purpose of carrying aircraft would be a lengthy and costly business, the British did the next best thing. They converted existing ships from which airplanes could operate, and the result was the appearance of some remarkably shaped ships.

Among the first to be converted was the British liner *Campania*, which had a tilted 'flying-off' deck added to the forward part of the ship. From this deck, seaplanes could be launched by means of wheeled dollies. Having completed their mission, the seaplanes had to be hoisted back on to the ship by crane.

The cross-channel steamer *Manxman* was also commandeered by the Royal Navy and fitted out as a seaplane carrier. Like *Campania*, her flying-off deck was located forward of the bridge, but she

The cross-channel steamer Manxman carried passengers to and from France until the First World War, when she was converted to a seaplane carrier. Equipped with two hangars, her flying-off deck was mounted above the forward part of the ship. She was also equipped with cranes for lifting the seaplanes back on to the ship.

Around the beginning of the First World War, the potential of the aeroplane as both a reconnaissance and attack weapon was realized. Both the British navy and the navies of other sea powers recognized that the new-fangled flying machine could be of use to them, particularly in the role of forward scout giving early warning of enemy fleet positions and movements. This realization prompted the invention of the aircraft carrier.

In 1917, the British cruiser HMS Furious was converted to a carrier. Her forward deck was for 'flying-off' and the after deck for 'flying-on.' This meant that aircraft had to be manoeuvred around the superstructure from one deck to the other after a flight. Furious was also equipped to take airships.

Furious

Argus

had built on to her two hangars to accommodate her seaplanes.

Towards the end of the war conventional aircraft were used from carriers and the cruiser HMS *Furious* was converted for the task. She had both a flying-on and a flying-off deck, located respectively in front of and behind the bridge and main superstructure. The siting of these flight decks posed a problem. An aircraft which had taken off and later landed had to be manoeuvred around the superstructure to the flying-off deck before it could leave on another mission.

It was clear that the ideal arrangement would be a ship with a long, flat top which aircraft could both take off from and land on. To facilitate this, ships were converted into 'flush deck' carriers. The first of these new carriers was the *Argus*, formerly an Italian passenger liner, to which was added a long, flat top. This addition gave her a peculiar appearance, and because of this she was soon dubbed the 'flat iron.'

The aircraft carriers which evolved from ships like *Argus* and took part in the Second World War are well known. But at the beginning of the Second World War these carriers were in short supply and they were desperately needed for convoy protection against U-boats and aerial attack on this vital Allied supply line. Since the existing carriers were involved in other vital operations, another form of air protection was devised. Certain merchantmen, known as Catapult Armed Merchant ships, had fighter-launching catapults installed on them.

Catapult Armed Merchant Ship

A fighter, usually of the Hurricane type, could be launched from the ramp when air attack on the convoy threatened. However, this had its drawbacks. Invariably the launch occurred far from land, and this meant that the fighter pilot had to bale out of his aircraft and be picked up by the convoy after his mission — a venture which proved costly in aircraft.

The coming of the hovercraft has inspired American ship designers to propose incorporating the air cushion system into aircraft carriers of the future. They claim that such a vessel could attain speeds of up to 100 knots, so fast that if a crewman stood on the flight deck he would be cast overboard. It is difficult to imagine an aircraft carrier travelling at such a speed — but then, not so long ago, men scoffed at the very idea of airplanes taking off from ships at all. Who knows what the future holds?

To counter Germany's long-range bomber and reconnaissance aircraft operating against Allied convoys in the Second World War, Catapult Armed Merchant (CAM) ships were introduced into convoys. Catapult launching devices were fitted to these ships; when an aerial attack came, the Hurricane fighter was launched to intercept the raider. The fighter pilot parachuted into the sea near the convoy when his mission was complete.

Crazy Craft

Connector

Of all the odd ships, the Connector must be without peer. Built in the 1850s by 'The Jointed Ship Company' of London, details of her exact design are not on record. It is thought that she was built in three hinged sections to 'ride' the waves more easily. Said to have been used as a collier, her three sections could come apart for the speedy discharge of cargo.

The latter half of the 19th century was the great era of invention. Shipbuilders and designers both in America and Europe made great strides in ship and boat development. But with these technological advances came an inevitable crop of freaks; boats, ships and maritime machinery born in the minds of men who dreamed of revolutionizing sea travel with weird new ideas in design.

Countless hundreds of strange craft were patented on both sides of the Atlantic; few ever got further than the drawing board, and those that did failed to either sail or go into production.

It is easy to label these inventors of that Victorian era as simple-minded crackpots. But this would be unjust. They were serious-minded men who genuinely wished to overcome a problem or make some new contribution to the advancement of maritime knowledge. Many of the really great inventors were at some point in their careers regarded as hair-brained.

Such 'gems' as the Connector made their appearance in the 1850s. It is believed that the Connector was built in three parts and hinged together so that it could 'ride' the waves and lessen the chance of breaking its back in heavy seas.

Surf boat

The circular surf boat, patented in 1870 by American Richard Tucker, had a convex upper and lower surface and was propelled by the use of compressed air contained between the surfaces. A series of air nozzles, jutting toward the stern between each of the several keels, thrust the boat across the water.

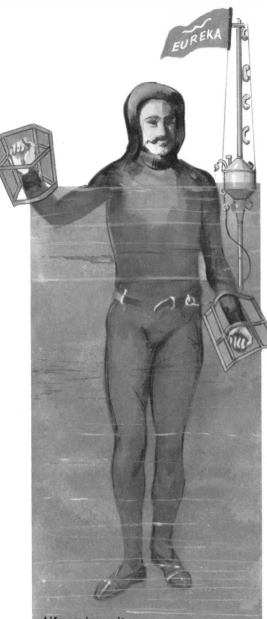

Oscillating sofa

This rubber life-saving suit was actually demonstrated in 1869 in America. A life-jacket inside the suit provided buoyancy, while a floating container attached to the suit held food, drinking water, a flashlight, distress rockets — as well as a pipe, tobacco and newspapers to read to avoid boredom.

This oscillating sofa was invented in 1870 by a man called Newell to overcome the rigors of sea-sickness. The sofa, supported on swinging hangers, is said to have remained stable despite the rolling and pitching of the ship. But the idea did not catch on.

American Richard Tucker's circular *surf boat* needed several keels to prevent it spinning like a top when it took to the water. Its method of propulsion was novel, too, for it relied upon jets of compressed air to drive it across the water.

This particular age was the hey-day of the velocipede, or cycle, in its many

Our sectional drawing shows another invention designed to prevent sea-sickness. In 1874 Mr. H. Bessemer reasoned that by installing a special hydraulic stabilizing apparatus, the saloon, which was 'free riding,' would remain level in all weathers. It did not work when fitted into a ship.

Life-saving suit

'Free riding' saloon

1877 saw the invention of a novel form of water travel. Known as the hydraulic railway locomotive, this craft required a steady flow of current in the specially-constructed waterway. The water turned the paddles so that the craft could travel upstream while supported on wheels running along rails on the rim of the waterway.

Hydraulic railway locomotive

Looking more like a space-suit than a life-saving device, the life-preserver, invented by American Traugott Beek in 1877, was made of sailcloth fixed to circular metal tubes. Waterproof trousers and gumboots encased in metal bands provided protection against rocks and attacking fish. Within the top portion was a month's supply of food. In the event of foul weather, the wearer could close the hood and breathe through the curved pipe.

shapes and forms. It went without saying that someone would attempt to marry the cycle to the boat — and one such oddity was the *velocipede boat*. This craft was propelled by a paddle pedalled by a crewman. To add a touch of elegance to it, the working mechanism was housed inside a gigantic wooden swan!

Throughout this period there was an almost obsessional desire on the part of inventors to deviate from the conventional ship shape. Some extraordinary designs were created, like the *ship on wheels*, which was the brain-child of a French designer. Each of the great 50-foot high wheels, driven by a steam

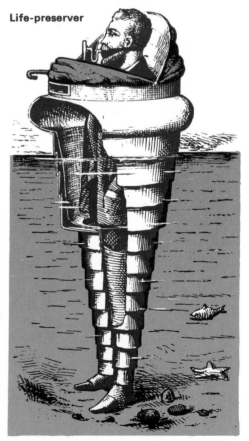

Life-preserver

Claimed to be 'an improved swimming device,' this strange contraption probably required greater effort to drive it than was needed for normal swimming. It was an American invention of 1880 and its originator claimed the swimmer could achieve speeds of up to 6 mph.

'Improved swimming device'

engine, was hollow and kept the ship's platform deck clear of the waves. Work actually began on building this grotesque sea creature, but it is unlikely that she was ever launched.

Safety at sea prompted inventors to dream up many life-saving devices, generally in the form of protective suits equipped with some unusual additional equipment, such as current copies of newspapers with which to pass the time until rescue! One of these suits, the *life preserver*, might have been better used as a suit of armor, fashioned as it was out of rings of metal. Another, although it afforded no protection whatsoever for the shipwrecked mariner, did incorporate forms of propulsion and a small sail

to help him on his way, together with a light to attract the attention of passing ships.

The prevention of sea-sickness was one factor which prompted inventors to

Before the opening of the Panama Canal, a novel idea was conceived for transporting ships overland between the two great oceans, the Pacific and Atlantic. It was thought that, if mounted on a giant sled, a steamer could be pulled across the isthmus by several locomotives. The idea was born in 1884 but never put into practice.

This elegant pleasure craft, known as the velocipede boat, originated in Boston in 1881. The power unit was housed inside the swan on the deck and the boat was propelled by paddles pedalled by the crewman. Directional control was achieved by pulling on wires attached to the rudder between the twin hulls.

Velocipede boat

Designed by a Monsieur Bazin, the ship on wheels consisted of a platform supported by eight gigantic wheels driven by steam engines. The hollow wheels provided buoyancy for the platform, which was raised some 20 feet above the water. Passengers and cargo were housed in deckhouses. Work began on this ship in France in 1890, but it is unlikely that she was ever completed.

produce some of the classic oddities of the time. Rather than attempt to stabilize the entire ship, they tended to concentrate upon a particular part of it — or even a unit of furniture. In 1874, a Mr. Bessemer designed and installed a 'free riding' saloon in a passenger ship. The whole room was quite independent of the rest of the ship and was planned to remain stable even in the roughest weather. Alas, when put to the test, it failed to perform satisfactorily.

On a smaller scale, an inventor called Newell devised the *oscillating sofa*, which rode on hangers. In rough weather, passengers could retire to their cabins and enjoy a stable ride. But this idea too had its problems and was discarded.

The day of the sailing ship was all but over, and steam propulsion had come to stay. But among the inventors there were still those who sought fresh and better means of driving ships. An American inventor called Chapman was one of these revolutionaries . . .

Ship on wheels

The locomotive was the fastest form of travel at the time, and it seemed not unreasonable to Chapman that it could be harnessed to propel a ship and increase its speed. Only three years before the end of the century he drew up plans for his *roller vessel*. Two electrically-driven locomotives ran on rails housed within two great drums at either end of the ship. The forward movement of the locomotives turned the wheels, which acted as paddles and drove the ship. Chapman's enthusiasm for the project knew no bounds, and it even received recognition in a scientific journal. But the vessel itself was never built.

The age of great invention did not end abruptly with the turn of the century, but rather it tailed off slowly. In 1925,

Propeller-driven life-buoy

In a bid to help sailors in distress at sea, Francois Barathon, a Paris inventor, designed this propeller-driven life-buoy in 1895. To operate the contraption, the sailor sat upon an inflated bag and used his hands and feet, aided by a small sail, to propel the life-buoy through the water. A battery-powered lamp signalled his position. The device was never put to use.

One of the craziest inventions of the Victorian era was Chapman's roller vessel, designed in 1897 to be propelled across water by two electrically-driven locomotive engines. These were housed within two enormous drums at either end of the ship. The inventor claimed that it could achieve the same speed as a fast train and cross the Atlantic in only 48 hours.

Roller vessel

another curious craft made its debut. It was the *Bachau*, a diesel-powered ship specially converted by German engineer Anton Flettner to incorporate two revolving cylinders, each 55 feet high and looking like chimneys. They were, in fact, 'sails' with a difference and rotated when caught by the wind. Flettner's idea was to provide additional power for the ship, but although the innovation did drive the ship a few knots faster in a strong wind, it got no further than the test stage.

Advance in science and technology has all but finished off the 'back-room' inventor. Changes in ship design now evolve as a result of exhaustive tests backed up with complicated computer calculations. The days of the inspired amateur inventor are gone.

Bachau

In 1925, German engineer Anton Flettner devised a means of harnessing the wind without the use of sails. Driven by 1000-hp engines, his converted steamer, Bachau, had two tall cylindrical towers, each 55 feet high. The cores of these towers were spun by the force of the wind and provided additional power for the ship. Although reasonably successful, the use of spinning cylinders failed to catch on with ship owners.

Exploring 'Inner Space'

In 1930, Dr. William Beebe foraged deep into the sea in his Bathysphere, a hollow metal ball which was attached by hawsers to a mother ship and lowered into the depths by this means. Beebe ultimately reached a depth of 3,028 feet, making some significant discoveries and photographing deep-sea life through thick glass portholes.

Sometimes known as a 'sea satellite,' the US Navy's bathyscaphe Trieste is perhaps the most famous of all underwater exploration craft. Unlike the conventional submarine, Trieste can travel only straight up or down. Her huge hull is filled with iron pellets and gasoline, which are used in raising and lowering the craft. Her two-man crew is housed in the spherical 'gondola' attached beneath the hull. In 1960, Trieste set a depth record by descending to 35,800 feet.

Bathysphere

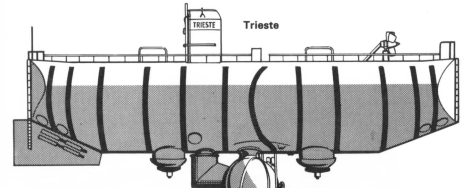
Trieste

Man has explored all but minute parts of the earth's surface. He has probed deep into space, set foot on the moon and photographed planets hundreds of thousands of miles away. And yet he knows comparatively little of what lies far beneath the surface of the world's oceans. Who can tell what mysteries lie hidden in these dark depths, what potential and unfound resources lie dormant and un-

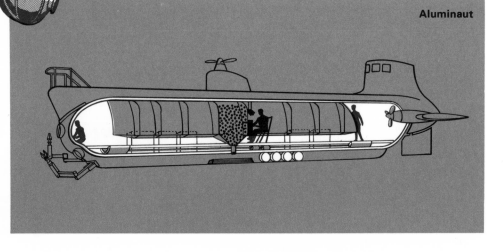
Aluminaut

The 50-foot long Aluminaut was specially designed for exploring 'inner space' — the depths of the sea. Fashioned out of light but strong aluminum, she can remain submerged for three days and crawl at 4 mph, while her three-man crew observes and takes samples of marine life and the ocean floor. This craft can work comfortably three miles beneath the surface.

tapped miles beneath the waves of the great oceans and seas?

It takes courage to venture into the unknown, where latent, undisturbed forces might lurk in wait for those who dare to enter their domain. But regardless of what may lie in store for them, there are men who cast aside danger to plunge deeper into the ocean to unravel its secrets. Men like William Beebe, Auguste Piccard, Jacques Cousteau and many others who have challenged the dangers

Diving Saucer

The ever-inventive Captain Jacques Cousteau designed and built this Diving Saucer, which looks more like an intruder from outer space than a sea craft. She is highly manoeuvrable, powered by two jets with movable nozzles. She carries a two-man crew, a battery of cameras and an extendable 'claw' which can pick up samples from the sea bed. Her maximum range of depth is around 1,000 feet.

Beaver Mark IV

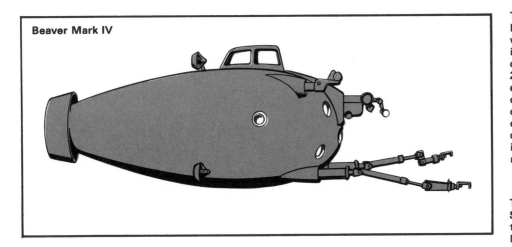

The Beaver Mark IV, a craft built by North American Rockwell, is a five-man submersible which can work at depths of up to 2,000 feet. Weighing 27,000 lb, she is used not for exploration but for carrying out repair work on off-shore oil rigs. Her protruding arms, controlled from inside the craft, can carry tools for making underwater repairs on the rigs.

The 57-foot long American Sealab III was specially built to test men's reactions to prolonged stays underwater. In 1965, three ten-man teams took turns of living aboard her for 15 days at a time. One aquanaut survived 30 days in Sealab at a depth of 205 feet without any adverse effects — but he did complain of being rather lonely and a little cold.

of the deep in some of the weirdest underwater craft imaginable.

In 1930, Dr. William Beebe became the first man to reach deep down into the depths to photograph and study sea life. He did so in his *Bathysphere*, an orb-shaped, hollow, heavy ball lowered from a mother ship. Making more than one dive, it reached the unprecedented depth of 3,028 feet.

Eighteen years later, Dr. Auguste Piccard designed his *Bathyscaphe*, which had the advantage over Beebe's craft of being able to dive or rise under its own power. Piccard carried out some important underwater investigations in his new craft.

Then in 1960, the United States Navy's bathyscaphe *Trieste* completely shattered all existing depth records by reaching 35,800 feet.

Since then some remarkable underwater craft have been designed, built and used for underwater exploration, notably those conceived by the Frenchman Captain Jacques Cousteau, who has achieved world renown with his highly impressive films of life in the depths.

On these pages we can see just a few of the oddities which venture far down into the mysterious 'inner space' in search of knowledge and discovery.

Sealab III

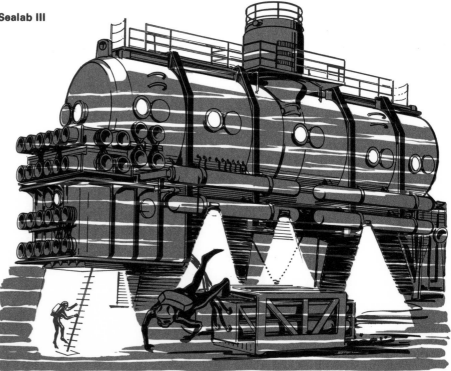

Paddle Boats

Steam Tug

Since man first took to the water in boats he has been filled with the desire to unshackle himself from the slavery of oars and from the unreliable wind. By as early as the first century BC both the Romans and the Chinese had designed paddle-ships. The paddles were worked by men or animals such as oxen and horses. The inventor Leonardo da Vinci produced designs for paddle-driven boats, one of which was operated by pedals.

Legend has it that in the 16th century a Spaniard, Blasco de Gerais, demonstrated how he could make a large boat move by means of a mysterious machine with neither oars nor sail. It is unlikely that the claim was true, and it was not until the advent of the steam engine that the dreams of the ship builders were fulfilled — at least in part.

Many attempts were made to marry the steam engine to the boat, but the danger of fire in the wooden boats often meant disastrous consequences.

In 1736, Jonathan Hulls designed his *Steam Tug*, which was powered by an atmospheric motor driving the paddle wheels. Almost 50 years later, a Frenchman, Claude de Jouffroy d'Abbans, achieved fame when his steam-driven barge sailed under steam power for 15 minutes.

Not all ship builders of that time were convinced that paddle wheels were the best form of drive for a boat. American John Fitch built his *Steam Oar Barge* with two sets of oars driven by a steam engine.

In 1736, Jonathan Hulls built his Steam Tug. It was powered by an atmospheric motor, developed by Thomas Newcomen. The steam was used to propel the paddlewheel, which was placed aft.

In 1783, Claude de Jouffroy d'Abbans achieved the then remarkable sailing time of 15 minutes in his steam barge, the *Pyroscaphe,* when he cruised upstream on the Saone, in France. Equipped with a steam engine, her paddles were located on the boat's side.

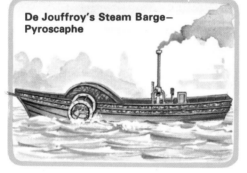

De Jouffroy's Steam Barge— Pyroscaphe

John Fitch, an American ship designer, was not convinced that paddles were the best form of propulsion, and in 1787 built his Steam Oar Barge. The steam engine worked a total of 12 oars, six on either side of the barge, to give it its forward motion.

Steam Oar Barge

Clermont

Charlotte Dundas

In 1807, the American steamship Clermont, the brain-child of Robert Fulton, achieved the distinction of becoming the first steamship to enter public service. She worked a passenger route between Albany and New York on the Hudson river. She was 142 feet in length and 14 feet wide. The accompanying illustrations show the Clermont's engines, which drove two sets of paddles.

It was not until 1802, however, when the Scottish *Charlotte Dundas* was built, that the great breakthrough came. This small boat was used as a canal tug and hailed as the first practical steamboat.

In France and Britain many more experimental craft were designed, but it was the American Robert Fulton who designed and built the first commercially-successful steamship — the 142-foot long *Clermont*. In August 1807, Fulton began a steamboat passenger service on the Hudson river between New York and Albany, a distance of some 150 miles which took 32 hours to cover. The service was a success and it led other designers to make great strides in steamship development. Soon they turned their attention to the world's oceans.

The Charlotte Dundas, built in 1802 on the River Clyde in Scotland, was used as a canal tug and was the first really practical steam boat.

35

The American steamship
Savannah, built in 1819, made
the first ever steam-powered
crossing of the Atlantic
Ocean. She was a three-
masted sailing ship with
steam-driven paddle wheels
which could be dismantled
and hoisted on to the deck.
During her voyage, which
lasted from May 26 to June 22,
she used her steam engines
for only 85 hours.

Savannah

In the mid-19th century, the
respective merits of the
paddle and the screw as
means of propulsion were
being fought out. To prove
which was the better, a tug of
war was held. The sloops Rattler and Alecto were lashed
stern to stern to pull against
each other. The screw won.

Rattler and Alecto

Built by the great 19th century
engineer Isambard Kingdom
Brunel, the steam-powered
paddleship, Great Eastern,
was the biggest ship of her
time. She was 692 feet in overall length and 118 feet in
breadth over the paddle boxes.
She had a displacement of
18,915 tons and was the only
ship to be driven by both paddles and propeller. In addition
to her steam engine, she could
set 65,000 square yards of sail.

The *Savannah* was the first to conquer
the Atlantic, taking 27 days for the crossing but using her engine for only 85
hours of the trip. Then in 1819, the
steamship *Enterprise* sailed from Fal-
mouth to Calcutta in 103 days, making
use of her engine power for only 64 of
them.

The great moment in the development
of the steamship came in 1837, when

the Irish cross-channel ship *Sirius* left
England for America with 94 passengers
on board. It made the voyage entirely
under steam, but the fuel consumption
was so great that, as she neared her
destination, all the ship's furniture had
to be thrown into the furnace to keep
her going!

Around the middle of the century
there was great rivalry between paddle
and propeller-driven ships. To dis-
cover which was the better, a 'tug of
war' was held between the two sloops
Alecto and *Rattler*. The propeller-driven
ship won.

Between the years 1842 to 1847, the
steamship *Driver* sailed almost 76,000
miles in a round-the-world voyage under
steam power alone.

The giant to beat them all, however,
was Brunel's 18,915-ton *Great Eastern*,
which bore six masts, five funnels and
could cruise at 15 knots. She was in-
tended to carry the unprecedented
number of 4,000 passengers and a crew
of 400. Her paddle-wheels alone were
56 feet in diameter. One of her engines
drove the paddle-wheels while the other
drove a 24-foot high propeller. But such
were the technical difficulties involved
in her operation that she sailed the trans-
Atlantic route only a few times. She was
finally relegated to the task of cable-
laying across the Atlantic — a somewhat
menial job for such a great liner.

Even today there are paddle ships still
in service. These are the magnificent
Mississippi paddle-steamers which have
plied the water of that great river for
more than 150 years. The day of the
paddle-steamer is far from over.

Great Eastern

Delta Queen

Admiral

In 1812, a passenger service was begun along the length of the Mississippi river in America – and the paddle steamers which plied that waterway were quite unique. More than 1,000 steamers like this one were built, most of them with their great paddle wheels at the rear. The Delta Queen (seen here) is still in service.

The new Mississippi steamer Admiral bears little resemblance to her predecessors. Although beautifully streamlined and capable of carrying 4,000 passengers, she has not the magic appeal of the old paddle-steamers.

Barges

At the mention of the word 'barge' we instantly conjure up a picture in our minds of either dull tub-like vessels laden with cargo being hauled along industrial rivers by tugs, or ornately-decorated craft towed along canals by robust horses. But the barge has not always been the 'work horse' of the river or canal.

Bucentaure

One of the most majestic and ornate vessels ever to be built is surely the Venetian *Bucentaure,* a state galley, or barge, used in the 17th century by the Doge of Venice on ceremonial occasions. It was 114 feet long and had 21 oars on either side, with four men to each oar.

For grace and beauty there can be few craft still in use which can match the Royal Barge of Thailand. The king's barge, known as the *Suphanna Hongsa* (Golden Swan), was built 200 years ago, fashioned out of a single tree. It is reputed to be the largest dugout vessel in the world. Fifty rowers propel this beautiful craft through the water on special occasions.

Centuries ago it fulfilled another more regal purpose.

In Venice, the Italian city of waterways renowned for its gondolas, there was once one of the most majestic craft ever to take to the water — the *Bucentaure*, a gigantic vessel embellished with gold ornamentation. This ceremonial barge measured 114 feet from stem to stern and was used by Venice's most illustrious dignitary, the Doge, only on special occasions. She must have painted a splendid picture, proudly riding

Suphanna Hongsa

along the canals to the cheers of on-lookers. She was a giant and it took one hundred and sixty-eight strong oarsmen pulling on 42 oars to haul her across the water.

The aptly named *Suphanna Hongsa*, or Golden Swan, originated some 200 years ago, and to this day is the Royal Barge of the King of Thailand. The skill of the craftsmen who built her becomes apparent when we realise that she was fashioned out of a single tree and is the largest dug-out craft in the world. With remarkable precision and timing, 50 rowers propel this beautiful vessel along the rivers of their native land.

Horse-drawn and motor-driven canal barges are among the most colorful craft afloat on Inland Waterways. In the 18th and 19th centuries, horse-drawn barges transported goods to and from major industrial cities in Britain along a network of man-made canals. Rail and road transport brought this era to an end, but now there is a resurgence of interest in barge transportation, both for passengers and cargo.

The American-built Thomas W. Lawson was a trading schooner with no fewer than seven masts. Although equipped with steam engines, they were used to direct the sails and not to drive the ship. Built in a Massachusetts shipyard, she was launched in 1902. Crewed by only 15 men, she had a gross tonnage of 5,218 tons. Built with a steel hull, she sailed for five years as a collier before being wrecked with the loss of almost all hands. Steamships were catching all of the trade and therefore the Lawson was the only one of her kind built.

Cargo Ships

Thomas W. Lawson

Oppama Maru

To solve the problem of transporting their cars to the export markets of the world, the Japanese Datsun Motor Company had the *Oppama Maru* specially built. Two driveways allow the cars to be driven on board and stowed below decks.

The container ship is the most modern type of cargo-carrying vessel. Containers – large metal boxes – are pre-loaded at factories, sealed and transported to ports by road or rail, then loaded aboard container ships by the use of specially-designed gantries. This method of loading greatly cuts down on-loading time at the docks and speeds up the despatch of cargo. Not an inch of space is wasted on these ships, as we can see from the illustration here.

For centuries, maritime nations have traded with each other, importing and exporting vast quantities of goods by sea in ships specially equipped to carry cargoes. For many nations, the export of goods plays a large part in their economic survival, so that without the ships to carry their exports or bring to them vital imports they would face ruin.

Cargo-carrying ships have assumed some extraordinary designs, ranging through the ages from the early trading merchantmen of the Mediterranean to the sleek and fast tea clippers which raced half-way around the world in the 19th century. With the coming of steam,

grace and beauty of line were forsaken in favor of cargo-crammed hulks that were anything but handsome to observe.

In 1902, however, there was one final attempt to retain sail in the trading vessel when the American schooner *Thomas W. Lawson* was launched. Built of steel and bearing seven masts, she had steam

Container ship

41

Five gigantic domes encase huge spheres containing a total of 125,000 cubic metres of liquid natural gas in this 936 foot long ship under construction by General Dynamics of the USA. With 43,000 shaft horse power, this ocean-going giant will make a speed of 20.4 knots.

A giant among giants, the tanker Universe Ireland has a displacement of 312,000 tons. She is 1,133 feet long, 175 feet in the beam and 105 feet deep. Yet, despite her size, she carries a crew of only 52. Powered by two steam turbine engines giving 37,400 hp, she can cruise at 14 knots. To appreciate her size, compare her with a typical oil tanker of Second World War vintage, seen alongside. Universe Ireland is a monster, but there are even bigger tankers coming into service, most of them built in Japan.

engines which were employed to control the sail. Sadly she proved little more than an impractical folly, and after five years' service as a collier she ended her days as a wreck off the Scilly Isles.

The more modern engine-powered cargo ships, although capable of carrying great loads of goods, had many serious setbacks, one of which was that each item of cargo had to be loaded aboard the ship *separately* by the use of cranes, then carefully stowed below in the hold. But in recent years a major innovation appeared which greatly speeded up this tiresome process. Pur-

pose built container ships were designed. These vessels are rather like gigantic tubs into which 200 or more big metal boxes can be loaded by the use of special gantries. The metal boxes are packed with goods for export and transported quickly to the dock by road or rail. It is then a simple and speedy process to transfer these boxes from the dock-side to the ship's hold, into which they fit exactly.

There are, however, ports which are inaccessible to container ships, but even this problem was overcome with the introduction of the LASH—'Lighter Aboard

Universe Ireland

Arcadia Forest

Ship.' This type of vessel, with its open-ended stern equipped with powerful lifting gear, lies in deep water some way off shore. Floating lighters, like the large metal boxes of the container ships, are towed out to the LASH by tugs, then hoisted aboard and stowed for the voyage.

But for sheer size, there is not a ship afloat today which can match the giant oil tankers, like the *Universe Ireland*. This monster is 1,000 feet in length and almost 200 feet in the beam and displaces far in excess of 300,000 tons. With the ever-increasing demand for oil throughout the world there would seem to be no limit to the size these enormous ships will reach.

Alexander Graham Bell, the inventor of the telephone, was among the first to build a hydrofoil. Here we can see his craft using the 'ladder' foil and driven by two aircraft engines. In 1919, it achieved the then staggering speed of 70 mph.

Ships That 'Fly'

Bell's hydrofoil

There are many factors involved in determining the top speed at which a ship or boat can travel, the major ones being its power unit and shape of the hull. Water forms considerable resistance against a ship's hull thrusting its way through it in the same way that air is an opposing force to an airplane flying through it. It follows that the more streamlined the craft, the easier it will pass through that element, whether it be water or air. Given a very powerful engine or motor it will be able to reach an optimum speed. But

There is a wide variety of hydrofoil designs, but there are in effect three basic types. 1. In the ladder-shaped hydrofoil, used in many early designs, the specially-shaped steps rose out of the water as the boat's speed increased. 2. The surface-piercing hydrofoil is acutely angled to elevate the boat as its speed rises. 3. Fully-submerged foils attached to 'stilts' achieve the same object as the other two types.

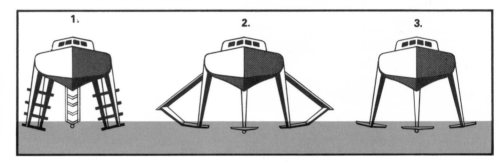

no matter how well designed, sleek and streamlined a craft is, it will still have to 'fight' its way through the water.

About the beginning of this century it occurred to men like telephone inventor Alexander Graham Bell that a boat could achieve unbelievable speeds if the hull did not travel *through* the water but rather *above* it — and in so doing remove the water's resistance altogether. The problem was how to achieve such an end. Bell, among others, found the answer by attaching aerodynamic 'legs' to the boat's bottom. These legs resembled ladders with each rung conforming

Hydrofoils are used in a wide variety of craft and in differing roles, but chiefly as passenger-carriers like this one, Flipper, which was built in Norway. The country which has made most use of hydrofoil ships for passenger transport is Russia.

Flipper

Denison

Hi-Foil 2

A superb example of the hydrofoil at work. The American *Denison* streaks across the water with her hull completely clear of the surface, supported by the hydrofoils. This boat, although 104 feet in length, can make speeds in excess of 70 mph.

The Hi-Foil 2 is a mini version of the bigger hydrofoils. Although only 9 feet long, it can carry two people and travel as fast as 35 mph.

to an aerofoil shape. They had the same effect as an airplane's wing; as the boat went faster, so the rungs produced 'lift' which raised the boat clear of the water. In doing so, the hull became free of the water and the resistance which had previously existed was gone. Now, given a powerful enough engine or motor, there was no limit to the speed the boat could make. Indeed, Bell proved his theory when he took one of his hydrofoils, as they were known, to the remarkable speed of 70 mph — and that was in 1919.

Bell's hydrofoil was a somewhat ungainly looking craft, as most prototypes generally are. But as time went on ship shapes improved, scientists perfected hydrofoil shapes, and more sophisticated craft came into service.

The hydrofoil grew in popularity, particularly in Russia and in the Scandinavian countries where they were used as passenger boats on rivers and lakes. Oddities like the *Hi-Foil 2*, a small two-seater with a top speed of 35 mph, showed their paces. In the United States of America, high-speed jet-powered naval hydrofoils like the USS *Tucumcari* entered service with the navy.

Tucumcari

The Tucumcari is an American naval hydrofoil patrol boat, seen here travelling at high speed. It is driven by water jets and powered by a jet engine.

Boeing test laboratory craft

But while there was considerable activity in the field of hydrofoil development, experiments were being carried out on a quite revolutionary craft by an Englishman, Christopher Cockerell. The result of his research and tests was the birth of the hovercraft. Like the hydrofoil, the hovercraft travelled above the surface of the water, but in a quite different way. By means of powerful fans, air was drawn downward through the hovercraft, forming a cushion of air which supported the craft and held it above the water. The air was contained beneath the craft by a 'skirt' surrounding the lower part of the vessel. But raising the hovercraft above the surface was only part of the problem. It also required forward thrust to 'fly' it over the waves. To

The American Boeing Aircraft Company built this curious craft as a high-speed test laboratory for testing hydrofoil shapes at sea. Bearing a striking resemblance to a lobster, it is powered by a jet engine mounted aft. The model hydrofoil is mounted between the two protruding prows.

US Navy SKMR-1

The United States Navy's SK MR-1 rides along above the waves on a cushion of air created by four fans which thrust air downward. Forward motion is achieved by two 10-foot propellers mounted in ducts at the stern of the craft. She is capable of speeds of up to 70 knots.

The 'Motor Cycle' Hoverscooter was an ingeniously constructed craft which made use of a 250-cc twin motor cycle engine. A single-seater hovercraft, it drew in air through a fan mounted in the front and directed it downward to give the craft its support.

achieve this, Cockerell mounted large propeller-driven aircraft engines atop the hovercraft, and these successfully drove it forward.

Since Cockerell's first hovercraft, the *SR.N1*, the hovercraft has both grown in size and adopted a variety of roles, ranging from a cross-channel ferry service between England and France, to the smaller military versions used by the armed forces in amphibious warfare and in commando operations. The hovercraft has one overriding advantage over the hydrofoil in that it can travel just as easily over land as it can over water. There are those who believe that the hovercraft will become the conventional ship of the future. Who knows — they may be right.

Hoverscooter

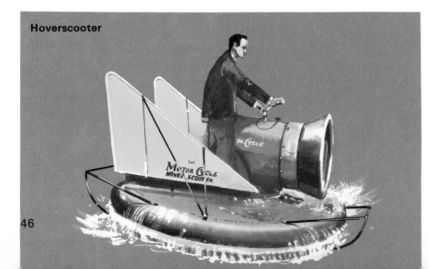

INDEX TO ILLUSTRATIONS